HOW TO GROW YOUR AVOCADO

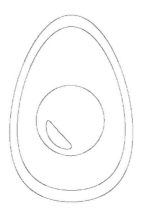

JOHN JUKES

For permission requests contacts the author. Contact details
found later in this book.

ISBN-13:
978-1974606016

ISBN-10:
1974606015

FIRST EDITION

For everyone who wants to grow an avocado!

CONTENTS

WELCOME!

Hello!
Welcome to the book.

This is very exciting!

For over 100 avocado seeds I have applied an amateur-science approach to predictably grow avocado plants. I've tried and tested different growing environments and measured some of the different variables including temperature and time to germination of those environments too.

So far the results have been extremely good.

Every avocado seed that has been grown in the method described in this book has germinated.
Every one.

Of course, it's not just about growing the avocado.
They make pretty good eating too.

Let's have some fun!

THE AIM OF THE BOOK

This book is to help you get even more fun from the amazing avocado!

Within these pages you'll find just what you need to prepare, sow and grow your very own avocado plant.
Amongst the key steps you'll find a few fun facts, recipes and activities to add more avocado love into your day! For instance, that picture below is for colouring in!

This book contains tips and tricks gained from my research into the work of other avocado growers plus my own avocado growing experience. I've planted over 100 avocado seeds and made notes as I went. This book shares the best tips with you.

AVOCADO HISTORY

The earliest evidence of eating avocado is around 10,000 years ago in central Mexico. Agricultural archaeological records show that the avocado seeds grew larger and therefore it is believed that the avocado was domesticated between 4000 – 2800 BC.

Avocados had significance in Mayan and Aztec cultures. The fourteenth month in the Mayan calendar was identified by the avocado symbol, known as K'ank'in. The Mayan city of Pusilhá in Belize, was known as the "Kingdom of the Avocado". The Aztec city of Ahuacatlan means "place where the avocado abounds".

THE WORD AVOCADO

Deriving from the Nahuatl (Mexico-region Aztec) word 'āhuacatl', avocado translates to 'testicle' - probably due to the similarity between the fruit and the part of the body.

In Aztec culture the avocado was believed to transfer strength to whomever ate it and also considered the fruit to be an aphrodisiac.

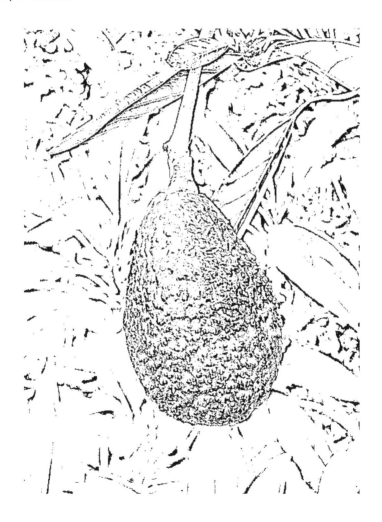

THE POPULAR AVOCADO

There are over one hundred types of avocado.
The 'Hass' is the most common variety and accounts for the
majority of global sales. All 'Hass' avocados are derived from an
original tree, raised by an American postman, Rudolph Hass in
California in the 1930's.

The rough exterior skin of the 'Hass' variety is tough and so lends
itself to long-distance transport as the avocado flesh within is
protected; this is the main reason the 'Hass' variety is exported so
readily.

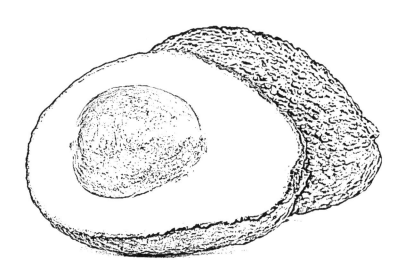

WORLD PRODUCTION

Mexico is the main producer of avocados.
The country produced 1.52 million tonnes in 2014, which was
30% of a global production of just over 5 million tonnes.

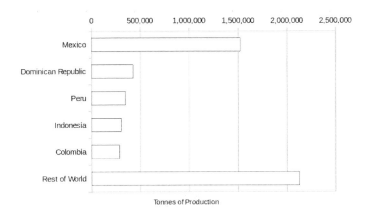

Tonnes of Production

AVOCADO STATS

The tree:

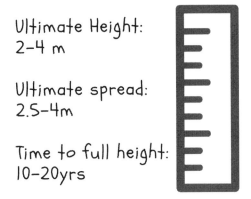

Ultimate Height:
2-4 m

Ultimate spread:
2.5-4m

Time to full height:
10-20yrs

The fruit:

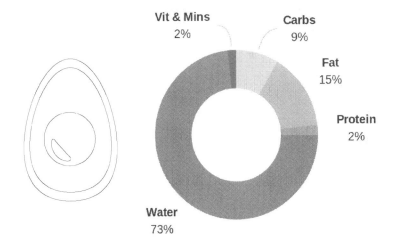

Vit & Mins
2%

Carbs
9%

Fat
15%

Protein
2%

Water
73%

THE GROWTH THEORY

So how do avocado seeds grow?

It is thought that the avocado adapted to suit the environment when, now extinct, Pleistocene (2,588,000 to 11,700 years ago) megafauna roamed the planet. The theory goes that the avocado seeds would have been dispersed when the avocado was eaten, moved by the animal as it roamed the land, then released via poo.

The seed contains persin, which is mildly toxic, so it is believed the avocado would have been eaten whole. However, there are no animals in the regions today where avocados grow that are large enough to eat and disperse avo's in this way.

Using this information I got to thinking; the avocado seed must need warmth and nutrients to sprout effectively. And, if the avo seed was in poo, then it wouldn't need sunlight.

The 'all over the place' growth method for avo seeds is the 'toothpick method'. Essentially, stab three cocktail sticks in the seed to act as a support, while the bottom of the seed is submerged in a glass of water.
This method is not reliable enough and so I set about investigating more predictable methods.

To cut a long, investigative story short, I found that heat is the crucial factor, closely followed by nutrients. Avocado seeds will germinate in the dark, so long as they are given warmth and nutrients (compost). The sprouts from the top look like albino avocados, until they are given sunlight, at which point they will darken to their regular green colour.

So, why is the toothpick method so prevalent? Probably because this method is used in America, where there are more people to share that method. And, because America is generally a warm place (especially where avo's naturally grow) the seed gets plenty of warmth to trigger germination. The method is also more fun, as it's possible to watch the root break through the seed – if it's sat in compost you have to manually check.

So – the secret for predictable avocado growth is warmth and nutrients!

GROWTH ENVIRONMENT

To grow your avocado seed you'll need to mimic the conditions in Mexico, or California. You won't need to break out the tequila but you will need to make a warm and sunny space. The warmth element is most important for seed germination, light is important for subsequent plant growth.

If you have a conservatory or greenhouse then that is ideal. They are natural sun-traps and keep in the heat. Second to that is a mini greenhouse, i.e. a seed tray or plant pot with a plastic cover – the plastic cover will help trap the warmth and moisture. Alternatively, find somewhere warm in your house as a makeshift incubator. A sunny spot on the windowsill can work.
A warm space with a little airflow is ideal, to prevent the seed from becoming mouldy.

Many of my batches have been grown in an airing cupboard, where the hot water tank keeps the temperature in the cupboard at around 20 – 25DegC. Remember, for germination your avo seed won't need light, so get creative when you consider a warm space to get the seed growing.

If the growing spot is too cool and moist then the seed is likely to become mouldy and rot.

COMPOST PREPARATION

Many sources say that regular compost can be used to grow avocados. However, I have found that a unique blend keeps the plants really healthy. The mix is well draining and marginally acidic as some sources suggest this helps plant growth.

Mix together one third each of
- Houseplant compost
- Ericaceous compost
- Cactus compost

Moisten with rain water when ready to use for planting, ideally at room temperature so as not to cool the soil.

Keep your compost in a dry container to prevent other things taking residence!

CHOOSING AN AVO

There is a bit of a knack to choosing an avocado that is ready to eat.
There are a mixture of checks, some are more reliable than others. I find that the best way to check an avocado is to give it a squeeze.

If it feels very firm then it's not ripe yet.
If it gives a little under pressure then it's probably good to eat.
If the avocado is mushy then it's probably started to rot inside.

When cut in half an early or ripe avocado will be a fresh yellow and green colour inside. An over-ripe avocado will have black marks inside as the flesh has started to degrade and become more fibrous.

Avocados only ripen once picked, so they will continue to ripen on the shelf as it were. A firm avocado is best left on the counter top until it has ripened, then placed in the fridge if you don't intend to eat it immediately. However, it's best to avoid refrigerating avocados. If you put an unripe avocado in the fridge then it is likely to degrade rather than ripen.

The ideal consistency of an avocado is one where the entire flesh is smooth and soft.

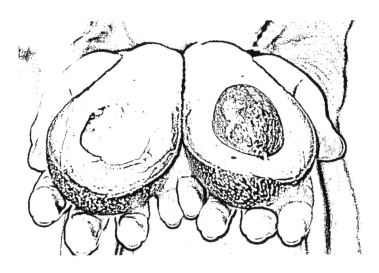

AVO PREPARATION

Take one ripe avocado.

Insert a sharp knife to cut the avocado lengthways. Press the knife in carefully so as not to damage the seed too much inside the fruit. Rotate the avocado, or draw the knife around in a circular motion to slice all around the fruit. Twist the halves to separate them.
Scoop out the seed with a spoon.
Clean the seed in warm soapy water (do it immediately – dried avocado is more difficult to remove from the seed).
The seed should be firm. If the seed is mushy or rotten then discard to your compost heap.

If not planting the seed immediately then leave submerged in water until you are ready to plant it.

If using the avocado straight away then do so! If not, cover both halves in cling film, pressing the plastic carefully against the surface to minimise air pockets. Avocado flesh will darken on exposure to air, so covering the surface will help slow the process. Place in the fridge to store for a day or so.

PLANTING

Prepare a pot or seed tray with a few inches of compost.
Ensure compost is moist. Water with rain water and allow excess
to drain.

Place the base of the cleaned seed onto surface of the compost
The base of the seed is wider than the top and has a white-ish
circle on it.

Push seed gently into surface of the compost

Keep the seed in a warm place and keep soil moist and not water-
logged.

The key is to keep the seed warm and the soil moist while it
germinates. A temperature of around 20 to 25 DegC is what I
have found to work well. This also lines up with what the Royal
Horticultural Society says too.

FIRST SHOOTS AND ROOTS

Once planted you'll be looking for the first shoots and roots from the seed.

The avocado seed may split significantly when the shoots or roots emerge, or it may not. Germination is usually between 4 to 6 weeks. But so long as the seed is not mouldy or rotten be patient. If the seed becomes mouldy, wipe it off carefully with a mix of 50/50 white vinegar and water.

The roots emerge first. To check if the roots are growing, carefully lift the seed from the surface of the compost. I usually check every 2-3 days.

Once the roots have emerged be careful to replace the seed into its original growing position to avoid damaging the root.

The shoots may develop at the same time as the roots, or some time afterwards. If the avocado seed has roots then do not be concerned if the shoots have not developed immediately.

When the seed cannot easily be removed from the soil because the roots have 'dug in' it is time to transplant the seed. At this point the seed may a shoot and maybe also leaves but not necessarily.

TRANSPLANTING

To transplant the seed, carefully loosen the soil around it and lift the seed from the soil. There is no need to clean the roots of soil enitirely, loosening the soil is simply to help lift the seed without damaging the roots.

If you like, you can trim the roots. I usually trim them, with a pair of secateurs for a quick clean cut, to a length of around 5cm (2 inches).

Half fill a pot (a minimum of 5" or 12cm is recommended) with the same type of compost mixture as used for growing the seed.

Hold the seed with one hand and rest the roots on the compost in the pot. With your other hand, fill up the pot so that the roots are covered and the bottom of the seed is about 1cm below the top edge of the pot.

Push down the soil gently to make sure the seed is planted firmly. Top up with soil if necessary, still leaving 1cm from the top of the pot.

Cover the top of the soil with horticultural grit or a small-grain gravel of your preference. This will help keep in moisture and prevent small flies from living in the compost. Water thoroughly and drain well.

Note:
The size of the plant will be influenced by the size of the pot into which you plant it.

As a test, I have grown one in a bonsai ceramic container. Such a container is shallow and rectangular. The roots become confined relatively quickly (and end up peeking out of the drainage holes). Also, due to the relatively small amount of soil, the plant needs watering more frequently than one in a traditional pot. However, the smaller container does slow down the growth rate of the avocado.

As another test, I have also grown an avocado in a larger pot, circa 25cm across and 25cm deep. The avocado was around 2 feet tall when transplanted from a pot of around 12cm. It has grown to 4 feet tall and the roots are just peeking through the drainage holes. The avocado also started branching sideways at around 3 ½ feet tall.

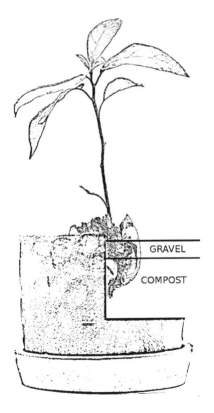

GRAVEL

COMPOST

LOOKING AFTER THE AVO

Avocados naturally grow in hot and sunny locations.
Give your avocado plenty of sunlight, water and warmth to help it grow.
Your avocado will grow, though at a slower rate, in cooler positions.

Growing slows in cold weather. Always protect from frost. My batch of avo's have been subject to 2 DegC and have been fine – but always inside the house.

If placed in a directly sunny position then make sure the plant is kept well-watered. While the avocado can survive short-term dry spells, the sunlight will scorch the leaves if the plant is in need of water.

The avocado should never be kept sat in water. The leaves of the avocado will start to droop when in need of water. This stage is best avoided, especially in hot weather, but use the response as a sign to give your avo a drink.

Avocado roots search for water (like all plant roots). They can quickly emerge through the drainage holes in pot. Either remove the plant and trim the roots, or pot up to a larger size.
Remember, the avocado will grow larger when it is given a larger pot to grow in, so if you want to keep it small, then trim the roots and keep it in a smaller pot.

FRUITING

I'll lay my cards on the table here and say that I haven't had a fruiting avocado yet. The plants I have aren't old enough yet.

From the research I have done, I haven't been able to identify any particular conditions that trigger fruiting.

Most sources suggest that it is just a waiting game, with that game including the application of plenty of sunlight and water.

The time for maturity varies too. Most sources say that the avocado tree takes a long time to mature – somewhere in the region of four to six years, although some sources extend this to ten years. However,I have seen one YouTube video that shows an avocado plant, container-grown, that is three years old and flowering.

However, avocado trees flower in a unique way. When the flower first opens it is female. When it closes and reopens it is male. For this reason it seems as though two avocado plants would be needed to ensure pollination.

Once pollination occurs it takes between six and eighteen months for an avocado fruit to mature to the point at which is can be picked.

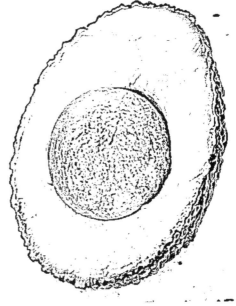

RECIPE: GUACAMOLE

Here is a quick and simple recipe for my favourite guacamole.
Most shop-bought guacamole includes cream but it's not
necessary – avocado is creamy enough on its own.
This recipe is great on its own. But for extra zing, texture or
flavour you can add: Chopped onion, coriander and chilli to taste.

Ingredients
- 3 ripe avocados
- Juice of one lime
- 1 teaspoon of tomato puree
- 1 teaspoon of garlic puree
- Salt and pepper
- 4 slices of lime to garnish

Instructions
- Mash or puree the avocado. Add the lime juice and
  tomato puree.
- Mix.
- Season to taste.
- Cut each circle of lime slice from the edge to the centre.
  Twist each slice and garnish.

RECIPE: FUDGE

Makes around 25 x 1" cubes

Ingredients
- About 100 grams ripe avocado (~ 1 medium avocado)
- 340g dark chocolate (cut into choc chip-size pieces)
- 1 ½ teaspoons pure vanilla
- 170g sugar
- 50ml milk
- 1 tablespoon butter

Instructions

- Peel avocado and remove the seed. Mash or puree the avocado until smooth.
- Chop the chocolate into small pieces with the vanilla and set aside.
- Combine the sugar and milk in a small saucepan. Add the butter and melt over a low heat. When melted, turn up the heat and whisk continuously until the mixture reaches a rapid boil.
- Continue whisking for three minutes at the rapid boil stage.
- Add the mashed avocado to the hot mixture, a little at a time. Whisk well.
- Pour the mixture over the chocolate and blend well for a few minutes.
- Line a 25cm square tin and pour in the mixture. Refrigerate overnight until firm.
- Remove from fridge. Cut into pieces. Devour enthusiastically!

RECIPE: PANCAKES

Makes around four large pancakes

Ingredients

- 1 ripe avocado (~100g)
- 100 grams plain flour
- 25g muscovado sugar
- 125ml milk
- 2 medium eggs
- A little oil for frying
- 25g dark chocolate (cut into choc chip-size pieces)

Instructions

- Combine flour and sugar until smooth.
- Add the two eggs and whisk until smooth.
- Add the milk to create a pourable consistency.
- Heat a little of the oil in the pan. Add a ladle of the mixture to evenly coat the frying pan.
- Fry for a few minutes on both sides until cooked. Remove from the pan once cooked and serve.
- If making a pancake stack, add dark chocolate to the top of the pancake that is first on the plate. The upper pancakes will melt the chocolate for a a melty chocolately treat!

RECIPE: SMOOTHIE

Makes around 200ml

Ingredients

- 250g apple
- 50g celery sticks
- 50g kiwi fruit
- ½ lemon
- 100g avocado

Instructions

- Juice the apple, celery, kiwi and lemon.
- Transfer the juice to a blender, and blend with the avocado.
- Pour.
- Enjoy!

GROWING YOUR AVOCADO

Use this section to track the progress of your own avocados.

Ref	Planted On	Location	First roots	First shoots	T-planted
Avo-One	3rd May '17	Window sill + plastic cover	5th July '17	2nd Aug '17	1st Sept '17

REFERENCES

- https://www.rhs.org.uk/Plants/21291/Persea-americana/Details
- https://en.wikipedia.org/wiki/Avocado
- https://www.thoughtco.com/domestication-and-spread-of-avocado-fruit-169911
- https://www.mapsofworld.com/world-top-ten/avocado-producing-countries.html
- RHS Plants from Pips by Holly Farrell
- 'Why People Fail at Avocado Trees' - YouTube video by daleysfr
- 'Growing Avocado : The best avocados to grow in your garden!' - YouTube video by Calirfornia Gardening
- 'The Perfect Soil for Planting an Avocado Tree – Amazing!' - YouTube video by VeganAthlete
- 'Growing Avocado Tree From Seed@ - YouTube video by Wis.Gardener
- How Does it Grow? AVOCADOS | A True Food Series – YouTube video by TRUE FOOD – How Does It Grow?
- My own journal ('The Journal Of John') and notes from growing avocados.

ABOUT THE AUTHOR

I've had an interest in gardening since I was a young boy helping my parents in the garden. We never grew anything as exotic as avocados, but I've always had a love of helping things grow. When I heard that avocados couldn't grow in the UK I felt compelled to show that it could be done!

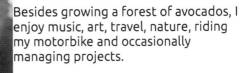

Besides growing a forest of avocados, I enjoy music, art, travel, nature, riding my motorbike and occasionally managing projects.

If you'd like to get in touch, drop me an e-mail at: JWJprojects@gmail.com

If you think this book would help someone else, then please leave a review of this book on Amazon to spread the avocado love!

To see some of the avocado seeds and plants that I have grown, check our Facebook page:
https://www.facebook.com/HelloAvocado/

Happy growing!

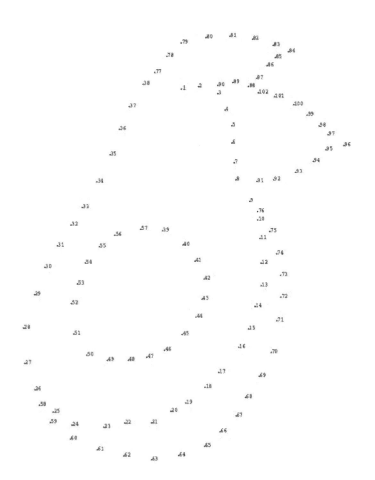

Made in the USA
Middletown, DE
22 June 2020